Tiny Homes

Tiny House Living For Beginners: Start Designing Your Perfect Small Home & Join the Tiny House Movement

Become Mortgage Free & Design a Cozy Living Space for a Minimalism Lifestyle

By William Walsworth

Table of Contents

"As you simplify your life, the laws of the universe will be simpler; solitude will not be solitude, poverty will not be poverty, nor weakness weakness."

- Henry David Thoreau

Chapter 1: Introduction

For more than 75% of the American people, debt is unavoidable part of their financial future. Regardless of how educated they are, what type of job they have or what their mortgage payments look like, most Americans in today's society are living from paycheck to paycheck. And truthfully, for many people around the world this is the cold and harsh reality. The unbreakable cycle of debt makes it incredibly difficult to plan for the future for most of the people in this situation. With mortgages and healthcare being near unaffordable, it becomes increasingly difficult for people to manage their lifestyle in a sustainable financial way. But what if there was another way? What if changing your lifestyle could make you as happy as or even happier than your current living space, without having to worry about many of the financial worries? Allow me to introduce you to my preferred style of living – A style that more and more people are adopting and is growing by the day. As a proud member of the Tiny Home Living community, I feel it is my moral duty to show you the possibilities of living in another type of home. One that is very similar to your current home – yet some completely different at the same time.

Living in a tiny home provides you with freedom, both in the mind, in the pace you live, and eventually also in your finances. Scaling down to another type of home has allowed me to make a shift in mindset that I could have never expected. My entire life I have lived on the countryside – a place of freedom and possibilities. Being close to nature and allowing my mind to stay away from buying many unnecessary materialistic objects, has provided me with the mental tools to scale down my living space significantly. The oversized and supersized houses of today's America are needless and generally do not allow for much joy and happiness. However, the coziness and compact living space of my tiny home has brought me closer to nature and a mindset of minimalism. It has freed up my mind and allowed me to see the world in a different, prettier way. This book aims to do the same for you – by allowing you to become familiarized with the Tiny House Movement and the do's and don'ts regarding living in a different type of home, you will get yourself closer to a more minimalistic and happier mindset.

Living a minimalist life with more of the bare necessities and less superfluous *stuff* allows for freedom in both the personal life and the mind. Thousands of people around the world have found a way to break the perpetual cycle of debt, work less and enjoy the possibilities of traveling more and worrying less. It's a surprisingly simple solution to a problem that has plagued the working class for ages. The best part is that you won't need to abandon all of the luxuries that you've grown accustomed to in the modern society, you just need to start thinking, and *living,* smaller. And by that we mainly refer to the size of your living space, because your ideas do need to be big to make this shift!

Enter tiny homes. These pint-sized houses are becoming more and more popular among Americas seeking an alternative to a life full of debt. By minimizing their expenses, they are able to live life to the fullest and spend more money on adventures rather than bills. Tiny houses really are becoming a cultural revolution. They represent a type of financial freedom that has previous been unheard of in the modern consumerist society. There is a reason that the movement of these minimalistic homes has only recently sprouted in American culture. The people in the Tiny House Movement are now trying to actively incorporate a different lifestyle, one of increased sustainability and minimalistic living. Ask yourself, are you prepared to change your own life and would you consider to join the lifestyle of the Tiny House Movement?

In this book, we will aid you in answering this particular question. You will learn the benefits and limitations that come with living in a tiny home, in order to see if making the switch is the right choice for you. We'll show you the building process and how easy it is to create a building plan that suits all of your needs, different approaches to the construction process, best practices for moving and parking your tiny home, how to optimize each individual room, tips and tricks to maximize storage space, how to install utilities and how you can live a sustainable, self-sufficient life full of more adventures and less debt. All in all a comprehensive introduction to what it means to live in a smaller home and how people in the Tiny House Movement decide to live their life of freedom.

Consider this your basic introductory guide into the world of the movement. Whether you have been ready to build a tiny home of your own for a while now, or you are still undecided if you want to make the transition, the stage you're in doesn't really matter. This book will answer some essential questions for you about tiny homes and help you orient on designs of your own, as well as provide you with valuable ideas on how to make the most out of your housing project. The knowledge you will gather in this book will help you to orient on your life decision, and help you consider whether a minimalistic lifestyle would be something you're interested in.

However, before diving deep into the many perks (and several downsides) of living smaller, we must assess some facts about how the ideas within the Tiny House Movement came to be. Furthermore, let us explore what the movement itself entails and if their motivations resonate with you as a person. Even if you can take only one or two of the movement's ideas into consideration within your own life, you could easily start seeing a shift in your own mindset: the freedom of having less and enjoying more is a universal freedom that could benefit most of us who are locked into our daily habits and schedules. It is exactly the minimalistic mindset that allows for freedom of the mind and eventually freedom of living as well.

Chapter 2: What Exactly is the Tiny House Movement?

The Tiny House Movement is a social movement in which people make the choice to downsize the space they live in. While the typical normal house in modern-day America is about 2,600 square feet (on average), the typical tiny house only sizes up to be between roughly 100 and 400 square feet. Another category of houses is considered "small", these houses size up to be between roughly 400 and 1,000 square feet in total. Tiny houses come in all kinds of unique sizes, shapes and forms. They are different depending on the designer's preferences, but they all have in common that they enable a simpler style of living within a smaller, more efficient amount of space.

There are several companies these days that focus on building tiny and small houses, which only shows what the demand for these types of homes are. The financial crisis and the aftermath of the hurricane Katrina have aided the growth of the movement lot. It is quite interesting to see how such tragic events have the ability to create a new social movement in our societies. Destruction does really breed creation in the case of the Tiny House Movement. The popularization of smaller housing continued with the introduction of several new TV shows, such as *Tiny House Nation* and *Tiny House Hunters*.

In other parts of the world, the growth of the movement can mainly be attributed to overpopulation and crammed living spaces. Where more and more people have moved to the cities in an increased urbanization process, the need for smaller and more affordable living spaces spread like wildfire over the last decades. All the way from Japan to Germany, and Russia to Brazil, people are looking to live differently. The opportunities have even led to concerns by housing professionals. With more people living tiny, safety of living might have become a real problematic issue according to professional builders of the homes. Most people where building the structures themselves, thereby disregarding most building safety guidelines. This eventually led to the creation of the Tiny House Association – A professional organization seeking for recognition of tiny homes in construction legislation. A serious concern because tiny homes still are not considered viable living spaces according to American law.

While there are a variety of reasons why people join the Tiny House Movement, the most popular reasons include financial concerns, the popularization of minimalistic living (as a countermovement to the consumerist society), sustainability and environmental reasons, but above all that the desire for more freedom. The transition in how people live their lives in a tiny house as compared to regular housing is tremendous. The opening quote in this book was chosen for a reason – living smaller really does allow you to see your immediate surroundings in a different way, as well as it enabling you to connect with the world around you much more intuitively and natural.

Tiny houses allow people to minimalize their living space, minimalize their debt, work less and travel more. There is a reason most of the houses in the smallest category are built on wheels: people seek to travel whilst taking their belongings with them. Why not ALL your belongings and bring your entire house with you? These tiny homes on wheels look identical to a 'regular' small house or cottage, only they are built on top of a trailer. This allows the entire house to be hitched onto the back of a truck and allows it to be easily transported anywhere. Whether you're trying to move to a new spot of land or just go on vacation without having to pack a suitcase, having a tiny home makes it surprisingly easy to see new places. The shift in how one lives their live in these homes is one of the key components as to why the movement is so strongly connected – only people who do it understand it. Much like you have people who prefer a hotel over staying on a camping site, it takes a special kind of person to enjoy travelling with your house on wheels. And it has to be noted that a tiny house is actually different from living in an RV or other motorized vehicle. The key difference is the ability to detach your home from your vehicle and change the home itself in a permanent place of residence with little to no modifications. The mobility of an RV is much greater as it is designed for travel, while the tiny home has the possibility for travel but is not necessarily designed for that purpose. It is a complicated difference and there is much debate on how one is different from the other in terms of categorization. But let's not wander off too much here.

The movement is currently at a size where it really is considered a legitimate way of living and is recognized by society as a possible alternative to 'regular' housing options. While the legislation is still seriously lagging behind (we all know our government is a slow snail that sometimes needs a little push in the right direction), the societal recognition is significant and the movement is still growing by the day. However, you must be aware that some people still oppose this way of living and are actively fighting against it. Many owners of 'regular' homes feel like the values of their properties are diminishing because of neighbors living in tiny houses. Yes, this does sound a little silly but it actually is a legitimate problem that sparks opposition among home owners, especially in the more densely populated suburban areas of America.

Although overall living in tiny homes sound great on paper, the lifestyle that comes with it is certainly not for everybody. In this next chapter, we'll look at all of the pros and cons associated with the Tiny House Movement. This way you can quickly investigate and determine for yourself if you would be interested in downsizing your living space and switching from a life of materialism to a life of minimalism. Is this really the right lifestyle transition for you? Are you ready to let go of most of your possessions? Let's find it out!

Chapter 3: Benefits and Downsides to Living Tiny

If you're considering making the jump to a tiny house, first let us take a look at all of the pros and cons in order to see if this style of living suits you personally. In this chapter, we'll go over some important things to think about before making the commitment to start building a tiny home and transform your lifestyle completely around.

Minimize

When you decide to shift from a large home down to a tiny home, one of the biggest issues you'll need to resolve is what stuff to keep and what needs to go. Paring down your possessions can be a freeing exercise that forces you to examine and analyze every item you own to determine whether you want to keep it. Because space will be limited and storage will be premium, you'll only be able to keep the most important and precious items you own.

The process of letting go of your possessions can be enlightening and incredibly freeing, especially on the other side of it when you're down to just the essential and most important items. Instead of your stuff owning and controlling you, you gain control and stay on top of the stuff. However, if you have the feeling there are too many possessions you should keep or are having a hard tiny choosing which items are essential in your life, it might become a process that is much more difficult for one person compared to the other.

The required mind shift for reducing your possessions to the bare necessities is a process that might take a while for you to sink in to be accepted as 'normal'. On a more practical note, it might be hard to let go of your possessions because of the value they have and how hard it is to sell the items you really do not require any more when scaling down your living area. Minimizing completely can therefore be a lengthy process that requires not only time but also willingness to let go of most of the unnecessary items you once owned. If you don't feel comfortable letting go of something, simply don't do it. Your lifestyle shift is your personal choice and there are plenty of external storage facilities that will aid you in the process of reducing the amount of items you own. Considering renting out a storage unit or using the garage space at people in your network (friends, family and neighbors) might be a good short-term solution. Taking your time and accepting what you need and do not need is a serious and lengthy process that could take some personal weeks, and others months or multiple years.

Design and Organization

To make a tiny house work for you, the design and organization of the space will be key components for success. Once you've pared down your possessions and you know what essentials you're keeping, start designing your living space that will house and incorporate these important items. It is not required to give up on luxuries – not even in a smaller home. Many tiny houses have shelving and storage incorporated into every wall to utilize this space effectively, which does leave plenty of room for all the items you feel are necessary in your daily life.

For example, wall to wall bookshelves add efficient storage space throughout your entire home. The kitchen will need to be a space with efficient vertical storage units to enable you to cook effectively. This means you must both be able to quickly reach the items you need, but at the same time find the balance to have enough room to do something like that. Vertical storage helps with this – by using the heights of your home you eliminate the need for much storage near the floor space (which is seriously limited if you live tiny). Another feature of design is to incorporate the outside of your house for purposeful uses, especially with the kitchen space. Many tiny houses include an outdoor cooking area for use when the weather permits. This leaves summer heat outside, as well as the excess smells that not everyone living under the same roof might enjoy. I personally like smelling my freshly made fries in my bedroom, but that might not be the case for every one (or for every type of meal). The details of efficient airflow is something that we'll discuss extensively later on in the book.

Maintenance

A large home (and all the stuff inside of it) takes an incredible amount of time and effort to maintain when you compare it to the very minimalistic maintenance requirements for a tiny home. With organizing, reorganizing, cleaning and maintenance, many people find that maintaining a standard home consumes a large part of the day – and a lifetime. With a tiny home, there literally is less to clean and your storage should allow you to quickly reach for the items you need. Organization will be a must to maintain order in this regard, but with everything in its place, your work will be done much faster. You won't have multiple bathrooms to scrub and scour and rooms to dust and vacuum. Essentially, the time you spend on the maintenance of your house is limited greatly due to having less space to clean and take care of. A great plus here for the smaller living space.

Living Expenses

A tiny house has reduced overhead costs, which should dramatically reduce your living expenses. While the initial investment for building a small home might be daunting for some, the end results are more than worthwhile. In fact, many people who have made the move to a tiny house find that they are able to live debt-free. This often enables people to work less because expenses will be much below average. Therefore we must see the transition as a long term investment.

People who do not have the financial abilities but are driven and experienced sometimes take on a tiny home project as something they are willing to spend a lot of time and effort into. With very little investment and the right connections (getting in touch with organizations and people within the movement is highly recommended) you can also build your own housing project in several months. Remember that tiny houses are completely different in terms of building requirements as compared to the traditional homes: general building experience and a driven mind will get you really far indeed! And the rewards are more than worth it, from experience I know it will even greatly boost your self-esteem when taking on a project this big.

Simple Living

When you have a tiny house, you adopt a new mentality as well. Unlike so many people who have a drive to constantly find new and better things to add to their collections, you know you don't have the space to buy and add more "stuff" in your home, so you spend your time and energy elsewhere. With a smaller living space, gone are the days when running upstairs to the bedroom to get something is a hassle. It should take you mere seconds to retrieve items or find objects because everything is close by and easily accessible. It's difficult to lose things when you don't own a jumbled mess of items, and with the organization of storage being key in every tiny home, this will come natural once you are living smaller. You'll have less to manage, so your style of living becomes simpler and less frazzled. The mind becomes free and you will be in touch more with the outside world, especially during the seasons in which the weather is helping out. It's like living on a camping site, except your holiday never really ends.

Smaller Carbon Footprint

If you're looking for a way to reduce your footprint and impact on the environment, a tiny house can be the ideal solution. The reduced size of your home greatly cuts the investment in heating, but it also allows you to buy less (since after all there is less space to put your stuff). The adoption of a minimalistic consumer pattern alone is amazing for the reduction of your personal carbon footprint. The reduced need for gas, electricity, and water comes on top of that: hooking op your home on the fly to these facilities allows for an increased awareness in using these facilities which are otherwise deemed normal. Automatically you will allow yourself to live outside more and connect with the world around you, thus also needing less electricity towards using electronic equipment (see the next bullet point for this benefit as well). All in all, by living in a compact house, you reduce your own personal sprawl as well as the amount of waste and greenhouse emissions you'll produce.

Time Outdoors

By placing your tiny house in a pleasant climate, you'll have the use of the great outdoors for more of the year. Expand your living areas outdoors by building a deck or patio area. You can use this area for cooking and living space if you add a grill, a countertop for food prep and furniture for sitting. You may also be able to add storage with weatherproof bins and benches. If you stay in one place for a longer time, you might even opt to begin a little area for herbs and spices, vegetables or fruit plants. Your own tiny homestead might help you to enjoy the outside life even more easily.

Mobility

Some people who embrace the tiny house movement opt to create a tiny house on wheels instead of setting up a tiny home in a permanent location. With a tiny house on wheels, you can set it up in different locations as the whim or desire hits you. Please refer to the Chapter on Tiny Home Parking for the details of seeking a good location (and the potential difficulties related to seeking these locations) for your tiny home. Follow the warmth and ensure that you're always living where it's nice and pleasant outdoors. This alternative technically creates a trailer instead of a house because you can move the house by attaching it to a truck. If you choose this option, research building codes carefully to ensure that you comply with applicable codes.

In the interest of being fair, there are also many drawbacks associated with living in a tiny home. If you're uncomfortable with any of these, then you might not be ready to make the transition just yet. The most important drawbacks to living in in a smaller home include the following:

- Space is extremely limited – you only own what is essential.
- You will not have an address - but you can get a regular P.O. box.
- A majority of your time will be spent outdoors and in nature (while this might also be considered a great benefit). Your personal privacy might be impacted by this fact.
- You will need to learn a variety of new skills in order to be more self-sufficient.
- The initial investment and mindset shift might be significant for most people, it really takes a personal change of mind to start living differently.
- Tiny home living requires a DIY (do it yourself) approach to home maintenance and interior design.

It's entirely possible to apply the 'less is more'-attitude in a real way to your life. Living happily in a tiny house may take flexibility, creativity and ingenuity, but many people find that this new and different lifestyle is a welcome change. Being mobile does provide people with a sense of freedom – and it exactly this free spirit that has helped to make living small popular.

Chapter 4: The Building Process

In this chapter, we will go a little deeper into the specifics for the building process of your home. Each and every tiny house should be a unique representation of their owner(s) and accommodate specific needs in terms of living, storage, and amenities. Visualizing your blueprint is important in order to get the process started – a great way to start is to look at what is already out there. Using examples and adapting these successful concept homes to your own specific needs is a good way to get the creative juices flowing.

Visualize

If you've made the decision to build a tiny home of your own, now it's time to come up with a plan. First, take a piece of graph paper and sketch out a couple of ideas including what you want the outside to look like and how many rooms your house will need. Create a visual of the size space you wish to live in, and have fun with it! Try building a cardboard version or a digitalized version of what you want and play around with what you think is best for your lifestyle.

Visualization is a crucial part of the brainstorming process, but remember, nothing is set in stone just yet. This is your chance to live the life of your dreams.

And important distinction that is made for the visualization process is between the floor plan and the actual building plan. The **_floor plan_** is used to actually design a technical sketch of all the rooms, both on the ground floor and the first floor. It will show the overall outline of which room will be placed at which location in the house, and where the largest furniture will be located. This will give you a quick overview of the possible ways to fit all the required rooms into your design and allows you to see how much floor space you will actually have after having set up the largest pieces of furniture. The rough floor plan will give you the opportunity to shuffle your design around at the earlier stages of development. It is easy to design yourself and when you hire a contractor you can give him or her the quick floor plan sketch you created. This will allow for quick and easy tailoring of the home towards your personal preferences.

The actual **_building plan_** entails the construction – this is a more complicated technical sketch of that include the walls, roof, and other building basics of your home. You can go ahead and design the basics for this plan yourself as well – see the section 'building plan' for more detail on this.

Identify Your Needs

The most important segment in the earlier stages of the process (pre-building phase) is to see which design resonates best with your own needs. What exactly will you need in order to live the life of your dreams? Do you love to entertain? If so plan your kitchen and living space accordingly. Do you work from home? If you have multiple kids, could they share one room? Make sure to create an appropriate office space. Remember that space will be very limited, so prioritize your plan. Adapt your tiny house design to your own specific purposes and if needed, request your designer to keep your needs in mind when creating the design for you.

Budget

It's important to consider your investment budget for the building process before getting the final blueprints together. Putting together a brand new home from scratch is never easy. The materials alone can be quite expensive, and if you don't have any knowledge of construction it is strongly recommended that you hire professional contractors to help you build your tiny home for you. Luckily, even the cost of materials and labor will be a fraction of the price that you might pay for a traditional home. Tiny houses have been built on budgets of $8,000, where there were no labor costs, to upwards of $40,000. Don't let those figures discourage you if you only have $10,000 and don't know how to swing a hammer. The great thing about tiny homes is that, not only do they greatly reduce the cost living, but they can be built on pretty much any budget. Even if you don't know your way around a toolbox, surely you have friends and neighbors who do. Recycled materials can be used to supplement plenty of store-bought construction materials. You would be surprised how many second-hand building materials can be picked up for cheap. As long as you're creative with your shopping, you have the ability to greatly reduce the cost of investment.

Building Plan

So by now you have a pretty good idea of what you want your tiny home to look like and how big it is going to be. Unless you have experience in hand drawing your own blueprints, it's best to find a building plan for your tiny house. This is a guide that will show you each step of building your tiny home, such as building a frame, installing a window, and so forth. Building guides still require some basic construction knowledge, but they are easier for most people to understand than a blueprint. A building plan design can take make shapes, but a general idea is to consider both the inside and outside constructions and measurements. This will allow you to end up with a basic design such as the one below. Don't worry about the readability of this particular building plan; this image is just to give you a basic idea of what a simple building plan eventually will look like.

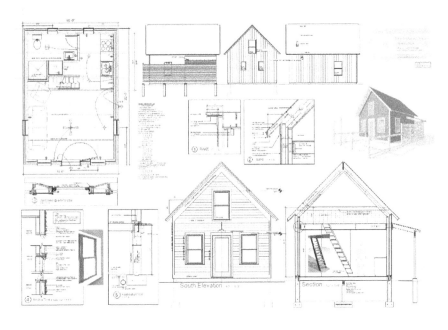

Image credit to Pioneersettler for this design example

You can also opt to design your own building plan with software available online. There is a lot of home design software programs out there, some free, some cheap, some very expensive. While professional designers often use AutoCAD, you don't need anything so serious. The same company offers a free, web-based floor plan design tool. A lot of tiny home designers have found Google SketchUp to be very useful. SketchUp is a free 3D modeling program that is not difficult to learn. With this software, you can design not only the floor plan but also the full three-dimensional design and details for your tiny house for easy use.

Although design software tutorials are available on the internet, if this is an area that you're having trouble with then feel free to find an expert who has experience producing building plans for tiny homes. Getting a really good building plan together is the most important part of building a tiny home and is definitely not an area where you want to risk any small mistakes, especially considering the amount of time and money you're about to put in. Therefore, please consider hiring a professional or using pre-made existing building plans as a basis for your own plan. A good design is half the work, so certainly do not cut down on investment in this stage of the building process.

The two most important things to remember before you finalize your building plan is to plan for the future and be realistic about the space you need in each room. Even though your final building plan might look good on paper, think long and hard about every measurement before you invest in the decide to start building. Furthermore, it is important to take an additional look at two specific elements of the house: windows and storage options.

Windows

When you live in a tiny house, windows will make all the difference. They open up cramped areas allowing natural lighting to extend an opening effect. Without sufficient windows you'll end up feeling like you live in a box creating a claustrophobic experience. You don't want to feel locked up in a small confined space: allow the daylight (and at nighttime the star and moonlight) inside and make the rooms in your home as open as possible. This also goes for the use of walls inside your home, please reduce this as much as possible to avoid any type of claustrophobic feeling. A good rule of thumb is that, as long as they are placed symmetrically in your tiny home, the more windows, the better!

Storage

This is why paring down your possession is so important. Look at what you own, decide what's important to you and plan where to keep it within your new home. By the time you're done with the minimizing phase, you should actually take measurements of the stuff that is going in your tiny home. With limited possibilities to store your items, ingenuity with the design will surely help you to come up with some amazing storage plan. Later on in the book there will be some great ideas and examples of efficient storage solutions that will help you with this design process.

It is essential to incorporate those measurements into a storage area within your floor- and building plan such as outlined before. Not only will this allow you to organize your space more readily once you move in, you'll also notice how open your space can feel with the right amount of organization. We'll go over a wide variety of storage tips and techniques later on in this book.

Time to Build

Never go it alone when it comes to tiny house construction. Organize work days in your neighborhood and ask your friends to come out and help you at appropriate stages of construction. It's a refreshing and fun way to fuel a build and interact with the whole community.

Be sure that you're building in segments. For example, day one would be laying the foundation. Next week, you goal will be to install your front door. Then, in a few months, your goal will be to put the roof on your finished tiny home. Never stray from your blueprint, and if you ever have a hard time with one aspect of building your tiny home, don't hesitate to call in a few contractors for assistance. There is no telling how long it will take to build a tiny home. It all depends on how tiny your home will be, how much help you have and how motivated you are.

The most important part of building your own tiny home is to have fun and enjoy the experience. Remember that if you agonize over every pile of wood you need to lug from here to there, it takes the joy out of building something that will last the rest of your life. Take your time. Whether you have contractors on your side or not, it's going to take a very long time, but one nail at a time, it will get done. If you feel overwhelmed at any point during the building process, just take a break and come back to it later. Sometimes taking a break from hard work can spark the most interesting of ideas. It might sound silly, but I found that going for a walk with my dogs allows me to ponder difficult problems more easily and it enables me to come up with great ideas as well. What I mean by this is: don't be afraid to take a step back from the entire process and overthink it for a while. Can't you just picture yourself in your new tiny home already?

Chapter 5: Tiny Home Parking – What is the Best Location for Your Tiny Home?

Considering the location for both the building and the parking of your tiny home is an important process because of the legal restrictions of where these homes are allowed. Most tiny homes are designed to be mobile and should theoretically be easy to move from one place to another.

Making your tiny home mobile has a great advantage and is therefore generally a preferred option. You get to enjoy adventures on the open road, see different sights and experience new things, but at the end of the day, where can you actually park your tiny home to sleep? This is something that every tiny home owner needs to be aware of, because all of the places where you'll want to park your tiny home is probably illegal. In fact, the only places where you can park with confidence are on your own property, at a friend or family's property, or in a mobile home park or RV lot.

Solutions are plentiful, however, if you are resourceful enough. Let me give you some quick tips to find good places for your parking. You could for example go on Craigslist or another service-based website to place a free wanted ad. Alternatively, you could opt to use your local newspaper to place an ad. Ask for a place to either build or park your home (depending on the building stage you're currently in). It is important to discuss placement of your home with local neighbors, especially if there are building activities involved. We don't want to cause any trouble in the neighborhood, after all. This also goes if you decided to rented your own piece of land for your home to be parked (either temporary or permanently).

Of course, this all depends on the local zoning codes wherever you might find yourself. Most zoning and building codes require homes to be a minimum square footage in order to be considered habitable. This is often 1,400 square feet, but if you're on the cusp, you should always check before you park. Often, codes will require even guest houses to be a minimum size that exceeds the footprint of a tiny home. However, there are also some accessory dwelling codes that allow tiny houses as guest homes in certain areas. It is a clever thing to never argue about laws or regulations with your local authorities and community. If you cooperate and are willing to listen to and provide solutions to your surroundings, realistically there are a lot of things you can get away with. Most local authorities allow for placement of tiny homes in places that are technically illegal. The main reason for this is that the zoning codes and regulations do not recognize tiny homes as a real living space, essentially placing them in a legal grey area. Be supportive, responsive, resourceful and willing towards your surroundings if there is any issue and you will surely be allowed in most places with your home.

Additionally, for homes with increased mobility, meaning they are built on a trailer and have wheels under them, there are different types of codes that apply. Mobility most of the time means that these homes are exempt from building and zoning codes. This is highly dependent on your local and regional regulations, and it is wise to consult these before making any assumptions on what you can and cannot do. Although you usually do not need a building permit to build on a trailer platform, your tiny home should still meet all of the required building code laws in your region. This is mainly to protect your safety and assure a high quality building standard. In the end, regulations are there to protect you, not to harm or annoy you in any way.

Many people think that a tiny home on wheels is basically an RV or mobile home, and technically they are correct, however both RVs and mobile homes were built by certified manufacturers who have the permits to do so. While there are several states which will issue a 'Home Built RV'-class license, those are few and far in between. Tiny homes fall under an entirely new and unclassified type of motor vehicle dwelling, and until the zoning codes start to recognize this, please keep with what is legal as much as possible. Creative people might even opt for a long-stay permit on a camping site. However, a backyard, rental piece of land, or RV-park are generally the preferred options.

Whether you're building a tiny home to live off the grid or just want an exciting and innovative project to work on with your friends and family, the best advice we have to offer when it comes to figuring out your city's specific zoning codes and how your tiny home can function safely and legally is to simply call the city and have a talk with someone in charge of zoning codes. In many rural cities, tiny homes are an oddity and the city won't know how to classify them, however, in larger metropolitan area, tiny homes are becoming more and more popular. You may have to have a building inspector come out to take a look at your house, but you'll find that once your city endorses your new tiny home, it'll be the talk of the town!

Chapter 6: Optimizing Each Room for Efficient Use

The size of your family and your traveling companions will basically dictate the size of your tiny home. It is highly recommended to keep the number of inhabitants of your tiny home as limited as possible. In this chapter, we will look at the best ways to maximize every bit of space within each room of your home.

Kitchen

The kitchen is where most of the messes in your tiny home will occur. If you make it easy to clean and organize from the very beginning, you'll save yourself a lot of headaches in the long run. The kitchen counter, in particular, is prone to clutter. Bare counters are pleasing to the eye and functional for folding laundry, unpacking groceries and food preparation. Bulky appliances such as microwaves, toaster ovens and coffee machines will quickly consume your counters.

For maximum space in a tiny home kitchen, find a home for any kitchen appliance that isn't essential to your daily life. Ask yourself, do I really need a microwave? Do I need it enough to sacrifice the counter space? Or, would it be simpler to warm my food on the stove? If you have two appliances which perform the same essential function, one has got to go. In fact, you should own some appliances that perform multiple functions, such as a pressure cooker that makes soup, steams rice and can cook a variety of meals. For nearly every type of appliance used in the kitchen today, there is always a smaller, 'micro' sized version. Adding these to your tiny home will free up plenty of space.

Store 'pretty' items high. Having high shelves or hangings baskets can clear your counters and harness the underutilized space above your eye-line. Put your 'pretty' items, such as festive plates, wine glasses or Grandma's pasta maker on a display shelf to double as art. Store your fruits and veggies in a hanging basket. Mount a floating dish rack over your sink. Hang your pots and pans from ceiling hooks. Hide bulky items. There's no room for bulky items in a tiny house. Place larger appliances under the counter when not in use, such as blenders or toasters.

You can create your own counter space by using a sink cover, or even a cutting board to cover your sink, making extra space for food prep. Eliminate the counter space allocated for a stove top by using a portable hotplate that can be stored under the counter when not in use.

This is a space-saving tip that can be applied to your entire tiny home, but is especially helpful in the kitchen: Mount items to the wall. Use simple wall hooks to hang your cutting boards. Magnetize your knives to a wooden magnetic knife holder and use magnetic spice holders on your refrigerator. The same thing can be done with the inside of cabinet doors. Mount flat or small utensils to the inside of your cabinet doors instead of using a counter utensil rack. If you have a counter skirt, sew pockets into the material for storage. Now every utensil has a proper home.

Food diminishes over time, so why should you store it in the same cumbersome box it comes in? Store your flour, sugar, cereal, etc. In decorative pouches or bags that can reduce in size as the food is consumed. That way, you'll know when you're getting low – because you'll have more space in your kitchen area. Very important to be able to cook properly and not feel cramped up in your own home.

Bathroom

The bathroom is usually pretty cramped to begin with, so why waste counter space with lots of different hygiene products and toiletries when you can find store them in containers built into your bathroom walls?

It is recommended to use wall to wall bookshelves for optimized organization in every room, although it works especially well in the bathroom because of all of the toiletries, shampoos, lotions, and toilet paper, lots and lots of toilet paper. Similar to your kitchen, applying fasteners on the inside of cabinet doors is a great to save on space.

Whether you have a sliding or swinging shower door in your shower, you can hang up a metal rack that fits snugly just over the top of the door, creating shelves in your shower. You can find the same type of shower shelves with suction cups on them that will cling to tile and plastic. Just don't put anything too heavy on them – suction cups can only hold so much weight.

Living Room & Bedroom

This is probably the room in which you will be spending the most time, as well as the location where you will be entertaining guests, so you want it look especially free of clutter.

When you're buying furniture, priority should always go to the functional pieces which double as storage containers. From stools to benches to couches and more, most furniture can easily double as extra real estate. Once you really get into finding ways to use all of the furniture onboard as extra storage, you will be surprised at how much space was there that you never even knew existed.

Is your tiny home built on a truck bed, or do you have floorboards with a few extra inches of precious free space? By cutting away a square foot of the floorboards (preferably under a piece of furniture, where no one will see it), screwing a hinge on it, then drilling a hole through one side of the floorboard and knotting a rope or piece of yarn through it, you now have a wealth of additional storage space that is perfect for those items that you rarely ever use.

The exact same thing can be done with your ceiling. Vertical cabinets that slide out are easy to install and perfect for extra linens. Just make sure you don't put anything fragile in your ceiling drawer and remember to lock them if you're traveling in your tiny home. If you have a stepped tiny house, you can take this one step further and add a crawl space or tiny attic.

Managing Your Storage

We discussed a wide variety of ways in which you can find extra storage in hidden places lurking in each room of your tiny home, but you may be surprised to find out that there can always be more. If you're really hurting for more storage space and you think that you have exhausted every possible free space available, then it's time to bring out your building plan and blueprints. Do you have extra attic space available? How about the space under the floorboards? With a little bit of creativity, you'll be able to find storage compartments all over your tiny house with ease.

The secret to maximizing storage space within one given area is volume. All items should be flat and flush against one another. Do not try to fit anything that is curved or awkwardly shaped in the same storage container, doing so will create a wasteful bubble of empty space. Instead, store all awkward shaped, round or curved items in their own special area. Remove excess packaging or bulky containers whenever possible. If it won't fit, don't force it. After all, we are looking for a minimalistic approach to storing items. At the end of the day, if you still haven't found storage space for something, then it's time to do a complete inventory of what you do and do not need. By clinging to the bare essentials and relinquishing the rest, you are guaranteed to enjoy your future home to its fullest.

Lights & Airflow

Most tiny homes don't come with air conditioners because they don't need them. As hot as summer might, tiny homes should be equipped with parallel windows to allow for ample airflow to circulate throughout the house.

In the coldest winter months, tiny homes should prepare every meal over the stove in order to generate at trap heat within the home. All windows should also be weather-proofed to help insulate the house from icy winter conditions. Double or even triple glass is a serious consideration with regards to this issue.

Chapter 7: Tiny Home Tips & Tricks

Efficiency is always the priority when it comes to tiny homes, but that doesn't mean that everything can't look as good as living in your new home feels. There is no better feeling than removing the clutter from your life and minimizing your number of possessions, but we completely understand that there are things you simply can't go without. Luxuries are there in a tiny home – do not feel scared to let go of the needless ones, however.

This section features a unique storage ideas to help get the creative juices flowing and inspire you on your tiny home journey. They will be supported by some images to get a visual idea of what we are talking about. The tips should surely be of use for some good storage ideas.

Space is one of the most precious commodities in a tiny home. If you have room in the loft to build in shallow floor storage, or anywhere else in the house you don't want to fill up with insulation, then why not use it? You can have pop-up mirrors, pop up clothing bins, books, hidden whiskey flask, you name it.

Earlier in this book we talked about some inventive ways to free up storage space in your living room. If you have a couch or any other form of seating, then turn the bottom of it into a simple storage space. For many tiny home owners, their largest storage space ends up being underneath their couch or another seating area. There are many creative ways to accomplish this. Top lift couches, side drawers, pull out basket, and shelves are all effective and easy ways to add more storage in a clean and stylish way. As can be seen on the example images, the most common options is using drawers and to place the couch itself somewhat higher than usual. This leaves plenty of room for all your items to be stored safely underneath your butt. Don't drop yourself on the couch too hard – we don't want to break the drawers underneath. On a more serious note: you could also use a stool as bonus storage ánd have a place to put your feet after a long day of hard work.

Most tiny home owners try to create as little trash as possible, but no matter how hard you try, you will still have a full trash bag by the end of the week. A large, floating trash can is not ideal in a small space, and with many tiny homes on the move, larger outdoor bins aren't always an option. When things are difficult, people tend to get a bit lazy and forgo the extra effort. So it is important to make recycling and composting as easy as possible. This is why it can be a perfect solution to have a hidden composting bin built right into the countertop. Alternatively, put it alongside the recycling and rubbish bin hidden below in the cupboard.

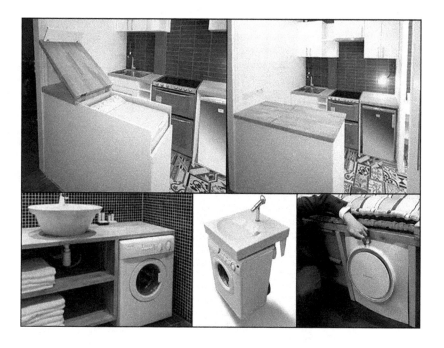

Having a washing machine in your tiny home is a luxury that comes down to personal preference and feasibility. Many tiny homes want to be completely living off the grid, in which case having a hand turning washer is a possibility, as is simply going to the Laundromat. But for those who are plugged into a water supply and have ample electricity, having the convenience of a home washing machine is fantastic, and for some people, necessary. But where would you even fit an enormous washing machine in such a tiny home? Many people put them under counter space and cover with regular cabinetry doors. You could even put it under your bathroom sink.

So you've found a nice place to fit your washer – now, how do you dry your clothes? Many people simply go to the Laundromat, but for those who can wash at home, you can actually build a traditional clothesline right inside your tiny home. Fold out standalone clothes lines have the tendency to get in the way, and when they aren't in use you have to find storage for them, which is never a good thing for tiny home owners. A pull out drying line built inconspicuously into the house can solve this problem. Alternatively, the outside of your home usually allows for plenty of place for a traditional clothesline. When the weather allows for it (it should be dry outside), placing your clothes on a line outside on the patio is a great way to dry your clothes fast. Just make sure you are comfortable with showing off all your clothing items to your neighbors (I remember my neighbor always had particular private clothing items hanging outside that we made some jokes about within our family). Privacy is always of some concern with tiny homes because of the limited living space.

Here are some create and crafty ideas. Many people have seen the tables that fold up from the wall to be used as a counter or table space, and this is a great use of space. Some furniture can be even more multi-functional. For instance, a mirror that changes into a lovely dining table and a stool that turns into a beautiful table that seats four. These furniture pieces are functional no matter which state they are in, and that is key for making the most out of your small living space.

Have you ever considered building your restroom into a closet? That's the kind of innovative creativity that is required of tiny home builders. Here, the bathroom is out of the way, there is standing space, and it actually makes more sense than having your clothes in the living room or kitchen. Some tiny home bathrooms are incredibly small, but for those who have allotted themselves a slightly more spacious bathroom and proper ventilation, your new closet could possibly find its new home next to your toilet.

There is nothing more frustrating then trying to pack a lot of different things into a deep shelf, and attempting to rummage through past multiple items to find what you want at the back of the shelf. This is even truer for homes where you are trying to get in as much as possible. That is why shallow storage becomes so incredibly useful. A cupboard with shallow shelves that includes more racks on the inside of the door means everything is easier to see and get too, saving you some frustrating digging. If your shallow storage is exposed, try getting creative with how you cover it! Like in the photo above where an old sliding door is used. Or, be minimal in the truest fashion and turn your shallow storage into art.

If you're not using a composting toilet, then it's a good idea to think about ways to save water. Even if you are hooked up to a water source, there is no need to dirty more water than need be. This unique idea of putting the sink above the toilet ensures the most efficient use of water in the bathroom and puts two of the bulkiest items in a bathroom together seamlessly. Sink water to flush the toilet is an environmentally friendly option that allows you to be efficient with your water usage ánd easily recycle used water that is relatively clean (the technical term for this type of water is 'grey water').

All photo credit to Melissa from Living Big in a Tiny House

If you're having stairs in your tiny home, you have opened up an area to get very creative with unique storage ideas. From cupboards, shelving, and drawers to hiding an entire bathroom, stairs can be your most creative space yet. Many tiny homes resort to a ladder type structure, however as you can see a regular stairway can also be extremely efficient – as long as you keep applying that creative mindset and efficiently use your available space.

Chapter 8: Tiny Home Improvement & Utilities

Most tiny homes built today are made to last longer than a lifetime, but just like any house, they require continual maintenance. In this chapter, we'll discuss different ways of adding utilities, maintenance, home improvements, easy decorations, as well as the best ways to increase efficiency, reduce costs and get the most out of your tiny home.

Doing the maintenance for your own home will require an abundance of skills. Whenever you can find the time, try to teach yourself a new skill or ability that you can apply to the maintenance or improving upon your home. If you personally had a hand in the construction of your home then you're probably already well-equipped to handle any maintenance emergencies as they arise. If you had contractors do most of the work, then it may take a contractor to maintenance your home when it is in need of repair. This is another reason why investing in your own handyman skills is so important. You'll also want to make sure that you have all of the tools you'll need for the maintenance or home repair jobs that pops up.

Before you leave for a long trip with your tiny home, it's important to walk around the exterior and closely examine any parts that could be loose, cracked or eroded in any way. Make sure that there are no chips or cracks in any of your windows. Pay very close attention to your tires, making sure that they all have the correct PSI in them. Go up to the roof and make sure that everything is secure and that nothing will fall off while you're traveling. As soon as you arrive at your destination, repeat this process for an extra checkup. This is especially important when it comes time for your tiny home's first maiden voyage, although it should be done with each long distance trip.

As we discussed during the building phase of this book, just like you can use recycled material to build portions of your tiny home, you can also use recycled material for both home repair and for decoration depending on your skill and creativity. In the spirit of being self-sufficient, you should always be looking for new ways to reuse items around your house, especially things which may otherwise go to waste. Reusable or reduced cost items should be used whenever possible. Get familiar with your local hardware store, second-hand store and interior design store and you will never run short on ideas to improve your house.

Decorating your home is simple, fun and takes little time and effort. For starters, you could paint your entire home in just several days if you do it yourself. For both interior and exterior decorations, look to nature for inspiration. If you have skill in wood working or carpentry, filling your house with handmade and storage-friendly furniture will cost you next to nothing and greatly impress your guests.

If you're living off the grid, you're still going to want to receive mail from time to time. Tiny homes don't have an address. This is why most tiny home owners set up a P.O. box at their local UPS stores. It's quick, easy and private. For the modern day life, an internet connection is a must within your home, be sure and find a place where you get reception from a cell phone tower. Today, any smartphone can be tethered to use to the internet on devices such as televisions, laptops, tablets and more. There are plenty of technical solutions that allow you to set up a Wi-Fi connection without having a wall-mounted connection from your local cable or telephone company.

In regards to your toilet, outhouses are a proven solution for dealing with human excrement, but composting toilets offer a solution that can be brought indoors, have all the comforts of the modern toilet, and are allowed in many rural areas. Another solution is a conventional septic tank or, where allowed, a biodegradable leach pond to dump your waste.

On the note of human waste, what about the other waste your home produces daily? One of the biggest questions on the minds of many potential tiny home owners is what are they going to do with their garbage, recycling and compost? While self-sufficiency is the goal, there are a few things which you'll need to rely on your city for. When it comes to garbage, it is important to first and foremost minimize waste. Always take a second look through trash bags before when they are full and ask yourself, what in here can be reused or used for another purpose? Next, separate all recyclables such as glass, plastic, paper, cardboard and so forth. If you have items such as banana peels and apple cores, those would make great compost for the plants surrounding your tiny home. Lastly, once you have minimized your garbage to the smallest amount possible, it's time to take it to the city dump. Some tiny home owners who live in rural areas use incineration barrels to burn their trash safely and without hurting the environment. With your bags of recycled good, look for redemption centers in your area that will pay you cash for the recycled material. Alternatively, many tiny home owners recycle or compost everything, throw away absolutely nothing, and generate zero garbage.

During sweltering summer days, cooling your tiny home is a breeze, even without air conditioning. While some tiny homes choose to use swamp coolers or air conditioning units, those tend to devour electricity, a commodity to most tiny home owners. On the hottest days, simply opening all of the windows in your tiny home will do wonders for your perspiration. This is why windows on should be built parallel to one another to allow a breeze to pass through your home and lower the temperature. On the hottest days, and when there is no breeze to be found, it might be time to break out the battery operated fans! Of course, there are other tricks to staying cool in the summer inside a tiny home, such as taking a 30-second cold shower or draping a cool piece of fabric over your head.

What about the frigid winter nights? We do certainly not want to freeze. If you live in an area that is prone to snowy weather, make sure that you incorporate extra storage onboard your tiny home dedicated to extra thick linens. First, if you predict a harsh winter on the horizon, make sure that you weather proof your window so that all of the heat inside your tiny home doesn't escape – these are also great for keeping the cold outside where it belongs! For particularly snowy regions, consider building a wood burning stove into your tiny home, or even a fireplace with a chimney. Make sure your tiny home is equipped with proper ventilation. If your tiny home is equipped with propane or electricity, feel free to use small, personal heater units when absolutely necessary. Lastly, if you have the fire roaring and the heaters on and you're still cold, use the most self-sufficient form of natural heating: body warmth.

Although some tiny home owners who enjoy an off-the-grid lifestyle prefer to live a simple life without electricity, have a source of power is a major concern for most. After all, what will you use to power all of your tiny appliances aboard your tiny home? While you can always run extension cables from an external electricity source, many tiny homes are in secluded areas, off the grid and away from such sources. Many tiny homes accommodate large generators built into the house, but you'll obviously want to monitor and ration the amount of electricity you use on any given day. The idea of using renewable wind turbines has been suggested and adapted into a few tiny homes, however, wind energy only works on windy days and has proven to be very unreliable.

One of the biggest investments you can make to your tiny home in terms of efficiency is solar energy. Investing in solar energy is ideal because it allows them to ditch outside electricity source or generator and become even more self-sufficient. Adding solar panels to your tiny home's rooftop should be a serious consideration during your initial building plan. Think your city is too overcast to take advantage of solar energy? Even on snowy days, solar panels are known to soak up plenty of juice. Once your tiny home is set up with an ample amount of solar energy, which you can buy and install yourself for around $2,000, you can use that stored electricity to power appliances, heat your water, warm your tiny home and much more.

Another big-picture question for tiny home owners – plumbing. Plumbing in a tiny home is probably one of the scariest parts of any building plan. There are many different ways to plumb your tiny home. If you only have a couple of units that use water, such as a sink and shower, you can simply hook up a fresh water source and run it through each. You will also need a large water tank depending on how much water you use each day, a water pump to maintain pressure, and if you enjoy hot water, a propane water heater that does not require an additional storage tank.

A lot of tiny home owners also use recycled water, or 'grey water'. Grey water is not necessarily waste, although it is the water that is collected in the sink and shower drains. If the products you use in the shower are biodegradable, then gray water consists of those products, your body oils, and food products diluted with fresh water. If you own a filtration system, you can separate and reuse the fresh water. Otherwise, grey water is good for watering plants and crops.

Chapter 9: The Green Minimalistic Mindset and Becoming More Self-Sufficient

In this chapter, we will discuss strategies to help reduce your carbon footprint when living small, become completely self-sufficient and even generate a revenue with some green homesteading techniques. Having a garden with your home is a great way to expand the area you use. Using container gardening strategies might even allow you to bring your garden with you if you decide to take your tiny home on a travelling adventure. We will go into the topic of gardening a little more here, mainly because it connects perfectly with the green mindset of tiny home living and the ability to live off the grid in your own living space using minimal resources.

If you're tired of making frequent trips to your town's market to buy the bare necessities, then you've probably already considered making everything yourself. Becoming entirely self-sufficient is a way of life for many people who have built their own tiny homes. Of course, where you live and what resources you have access to will determine which items you'll be able to grow and make yourself.

Homesteaders all over the world sell the items they grow on their land and the items that make from home. By growing your own food, you will be able to achieve self-sufficiency, better nutrition for you and your family, extra income and even your own homesteading business. If the land surrounding your tiny home is fertile then you should have no problem growing enough crops to feed your entire family. When selecting spot to ultimately park your tiny home, the quality of the soil should be a priority. Look for dirt that is most about three to four inches underground. If your soil is dry and dusty, there is no point in planting crops in that area.

The first thing to do when growing your own food for you and your family is to make a list of all of the foods you will enjoy eating most. Keep in mind the season that each crop thrives in, the time it will take between sowing your crops and harvesting and how much attention each crop will require. Will you need to spend extra money on things like quality fertilizer and an irrigation system, or can you grow a sufficient amount of food merely by watering them with a watering can every day? Will you have to deal with things like birds, rabbits and other produce-hungry predators where you live? It's important to take into consideration the total cost of sowing, growing and harvesting your own food from the moment you plant your first seed to the time it ends up on your dinner plate.

While crops such as apple and orange trees are good ideas as a long term homesteading strategy, the first few crops that you plant should be foods that you can harvest and enjoy the same year. Produce such as tomatoes, radishes, carrots, strawberries, lettuce and other fruits and vegetables are reliable and relatively easy to grow regardless of your gardening ability. Before you plant anything, research what season is best for planting what crops and when the best time of the year is to harvest. Once you have everything planned out on a piece of paper, similar to how you designed your tiny home building plan, it's time to make a trip to the hardware store to buy seeds and fertilizer as well as stakes and twine to build a small fence around your garden.

Only buy the items that you cannot make yourself. The last thing you want to do is struggle to find storage space for bags of fertilizer and fencing material onboard your tiny home. Some families create their own fertilizer from waste and compost, and the gray water that you've been collecting from your showers And sinks is perfect for watering your plants. You'll need to build a fence around your crops to keep out animals, however, search the recyclable items inside your tiny home before you go out and buy the materials to build a fence. Even after you've built a fence, be mindful of signs of animals eating your crops. Depending on what type of animals are eating your crops, you may need to build additional fences, scarecrows or set traps. Poison and pesticides should be avoided whenever possible.

Next, survey your land and decide how much space you will dedicate each crop. Dig trenches in rows for each crop and make sure that each trench is spaced far apart from one another. Make sure that they are planted in an area that will get ample sunlight and will be easy to water on a daily basis.

A majority of tiny home owners keep some form of a herb garden. Is something that can be managed inside of your house, on your porch or in a bed of herbs next to your other crops if you plan of growing herbs in large quantities. Common herbs, such as basil, rosemary, thyme and many more area easy to grow and a great addition to any home cooked meal. Many herbs can able to grouned up and distilled in alcohol to create powerful tincures that have a variety of applications.

Another homesteading tip you may want to consider is caring for livestock. If you have the land, financial means and time to care for your own livestock you will be able to produce valuable foods such as eggs, milk, cheese and meat for you and your family. A few chickens, goats or cows are an excellent place to start when it comes to livestock. The trick to successfully raising livestock is to keep the number of animals you own to manageable level. You should avoid the need to build chicken coops or barns whenever possible. Instead, keep your livestock contained within a large fenced off area so that they can graze openly while keeping the predators at bay. Cows and goats should be grass fed and milked by hand.

One of the benefits of keeping livestock is that you will be able to breed them on your own and produce even more food for you and your family as time goes on. If you plan on hatching chicken eggs as part of your long term tiny home self-sufficiency strategy, you will need to build an incubator. This is a one-time cost that will allow you to enjoy more eggs and chicken meat in the future.

Making items such as soaps, candles, lotions and balms are another great addition to your overall self-sufficiency strategy. The benefit of making these items yourself is that they can be made organic and free from many of the harmful or unnecessary additives that are in commercial products. One of the drawbacks of making these items is that that are usually made in bulk and you will need you find storage space in your tiny home for all of the ingredients and precursors for homemade items.

There are plenty of tiny home owners who have taken to homesteading in order to make an income living off of their own land. If you have a surplus of crops, consider selling them to local restaurants or even opening up a booth at your local farmer's market to let the whole community enjoy them. Homemade items, such as soap, candles, lotion, balms, tinctures and event handmade jewelry is a commodity in most local markets and easy to sell.

There are also certain types of crops that many homesteaders grow specifically to sell to merchants. Items such as bamboo reeds, oyster mushrooms, garlic and ginseng are all valuable in most local markets and can be sold at a high price. If you plan on growing crops to sell, be sure and check your local market prices first and, if possible, locate potential buyers before investing in cash crops.

Growing for income is long term strategy which will require you to obtain a business license from your state. If you plan on selling meat or eggs, you will need to petition for a Homesteading Foods license and the area you're using for a farm may be subject to inspection. Again, this all depends on what state you live in, as each region has their own, unique laws when it comes to selling produce, however, if your intention is to simply consume everything that you grow in the name of self-sufficiency, no additional license is required.

If you would like to learn more about homesteading and how you can earn money by living off of your land, please consider reading one of my other books titled *Homesteading for Beginners.*

Most of the people who have built their own tiny homes live on their own property for most of the year. There is a whole community of tiny homes who would love to do a land swap, in which two tiny homes park on each other's land for an extended stay and enjoy the local sights. Being able to share your garden or excess garden produce with other people within the tiny home community allows you to easily connect and network. A great opportunity to make friends and enjoy life together. Another advantage of being in the tiny home community is sharing your experience with others. There are plenty of tiny home forums online where you can meet other people who have built their own home, swap strategies, share stories and make like-minded friends. Off-grid living and green, sustainable minimalism are lifestyles that connect with most people in the Tiny House Movement and this is exactly why small homestead or gardening project is great as an outdoor side-project.

Chapter 10: Planning for the Future Starts Now

There has never been a better time to build your own tiny home, free yourself from a lifetime of debt and enjoy travel and adventure with your whole family. Although this book has provided the basics of the tiny home movement, there are still plenty of innovations you can make to your own tiny home in order to increase self-sufficiency and enjoy an overall better quality of life. Regardless of if the tiny home lifestyle is not suited for you, hopefully you have still found plenty of beneficial ideas and inspirations in this book to apply to your own life and home in order to start living a greener, self-sufficiently and debt-free life.

Thank you for reading *Tiny Homes.* Now that you know the basics of planning, building and deploying your own tiny home, it's time to embark upon your own adventure. Take the information within this book as inspiration of your own and start planning your own tiny home journey today. As you have seen throughout the course of this book, everything starts with a good plan, as well as being creative and resourceful at all times. There certainly are limitations to this lifestyle, but the freeing of the mind of becoming minimalistic and living in a cozy, small home with a nice garden outside is truly amazing. I can speak from my own experience, I personally lived on the countryside in a small, tiny home for most of my life. The discovery of an entire movement behind this several years ago has allowed me to open my mind to the amazing housing possibilities out there. I am more than sure that this book has helped you to understand that process of lifestyle change and minimalistic living options as well.

And tiny home living projects can be started with ease. Laying the groundwork for your future tiny home can be done in just a few hours. Start by making a list of everything you want to incorporate into your own tiny home. Then grab the free home design software, Google SketchUp, to come up with your own tiny home plan. After that comes the financial planning. Come up with a realistic amount of money you are willing to spend on your tiny home. Remember to consider all of the cost issues mentioned in Chapter 4 of this book. Once you know how roughly how much your tiny home is going to cost, come up with a financial plan to start saving and investing in your future dream house.

The most important step in preparing for a minimalist future of self-sufficiency, and usually the most difficult process for most people, is to begin paring down all of your possessions. Sell everything that is superfluous or that you won't be able to take with you in your new home. This step is often the make-it-or-break-it step for people. If you find it difficult to part with your material possessions that aren't essential to your everyday survival, then the tiny home lifestyle might not be for you. On the other hand, if the idea of ridding yourself of your excess items is exciting to you, then you are one step closer to building your own tiny home. Just be sure and save the money from the items you sell and put it in a tiny home fund. After all of your superfluous items have been sold off, you may find yourself already half way to reaching your financial goal for your tiny home fund!

If this book was helpful to you or if you enjoyed reading this book, please consider leaving an honest review. This allows other readers to make an informed decision on purchasing this book. It also helps me with the visibility of this book.

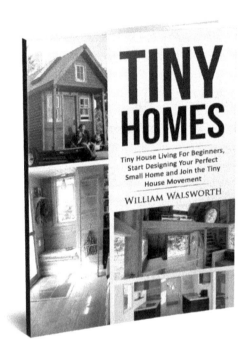

An honest review is greatly appreciated. By leaving a review you aid me in writing new content and allowing others to enjoy this book as well. Thank you for your time and for your help, and once again for reading this book.

If you would like to keep in touch with me and receive my future books for free, you can follow me on Facebook or Twitter. Simply type in my name and you will be able to find me. I always love to keep my audience informed. Thanks!

William Walsworth

Author, biologist & sustainable living expert

CPSIA information can be obtained
at www.ICGtesting.com
Printed in the USA
LVHW060315280623
751010LV00023B/409